Destiny Is A Matter Of Choice

By

Blessed Thabang Mobosi

Copyright Blessed Thabang Mobosi 2016

Destiny Is A Matter Of Choice

Destiny Is A Matter Of Choice

Published by

William Jenkins

2503 4288 Grange Street

Burnaby BC V5H 1P2

Canada

williamhenryjenkins@gmail.com

http://williamjenkins.ca

Cell: 1-778-953-6139

ISBN: 978-1-928164-16-6

Destiny Is A Matter Of Choice

Destiny Is A Matter Of Choice

Author

Blessed Thabang Mobosi

My name is Blessed Thabang Mobosi. I was born on 17 December 1997. I live in South Africa with my parents, with two young brothers and one sister.

I believe that my calling is to become a Financial Manager. I hope to study Commerce and Finance in university and specialise in Financial Management as a career. As well, I want to be an International Evangelist. My role model is Dag Heward Mills.

Destiny Is A Matter Of Choice

I am a minister and a disciple at Jubilee Christian Church International. I am also a keyboardist and an interpreter in the church.

I am currently the Chairperson of the Student Christian Organisation of Ritavi Circuit and I mentor about 26 school students under my leadership.

When I was eleven, I started to preach and motivate students at primary level at Ritavi Primary School located here in Nkowankowa, Limpopo.

I wish to reach out the world with my motivational sermons, poems and speeches. I have been invited on many different occasions to act as minister.

Email: Blessed.btm@gmail.com

Contact: +27 61 953 9726 or

+ 27 78 506 5555

Destiny Is A Matter Of Choice

Table of Contents

Introduction 1

Choices 3

Life is a Story 6

How Choices Affect Our Destiny 8

Have a Purpose 10

    Dream or Plan..10

    Be Cautious 11

Use of Time 13

Work Hard 14

    Commitment 14

    Measure Your Success 16

    Don't Quit 16

    See The Future 18

Avoid Destiny Robbers 19

    Motivate Yourself 20

    Mistakes 20

Who Can Destroy Your Destiny? 24

    Friendly Enemies 24

    Bad Company 25

Use Your Time and Money Effectively 27

    Time 27

Destiny Is A Matter Of Choice

Money 28
Seek Advice 30
Things You Need 31
Be Single-Minded 33
    You're In Charge Of Your Destiny 33
Why Some People Fail To Fulfil Their Destiny 35
    Fear of success and failure 36
    Lack of understanding upon achieving their objectives-setting process 37
    Lack of commitment to their objectives 38
    Stagnation 39
    Questions and doubts 39
    Lack of a real destination 40
    Failing to plan 41
    Having too many goals 42
    Feeling unworthy of the outcomes 42
    Lack of motivation 43
    Lack of consistency 44
    Excuses 45
Enemies of destiny 47
Fulfil your destiny 52

Destiny Is A Matter Of Choice

Introduction

According to my perspective, the word "destiny" refers to the purpose why you were born. The definition of "destiny" includes the events that will necessarily happen to you in the future. It includes the mission which you have to fulfil and the vision that you have throughout your life. Basically your destiny is what the Creator has decided that you will achieve. It is God's manual about your life. It is God's prophetic agenda for your life.

It is what is written about your life that has to be accomplished by you. It is the reason why you exist and you were created. Each of us was born for a purpose. There is a reason why God has created you. You do not exist by mistake or chance no matter what occurred when you were conceived.

There is something great about you. You are something that has never existed in this world. No one is like you. You are unique.

A philosopher once said, "We were fearfully and wonderfully made."

Destiny Is A Matter Of Choice

You have to be proud of who you are. Be yourself, love yourself; and have the confidence that you're going to make it in life.

Sometimes I wonder "What was the Creator thinking when he created you and me?" Did he look down upon the surface of the earth and say, "There is something missing in the world. I need to create someone to go and accomplish it"? With his wisdom, he determined the manner of person he must create and he created you and planted you here in your country.

Now that you are born, now that you exist and now that you are here, what is next? Who are you? Where are you going? What's your direction?

Destiny Is A Matter Of Choice

Choices

Life is all about making decisions, choosing one activity or another. The world is waiting for you to rise and shine; the nations are waiting for your arrival.

You may ask "I hear all about greatness, but how can I become a great, successful person? I come from a poor family."

Actually, where you come from doesn't determine where you are going in life. What you choose and how you live your life today will determine how you live tomorrow. Life is all about making choices.

The fact that you were born in a poor family does not mean that you also must die being a poor person. It all depends on the choices you make. It does not take what happens around you to change your world, but it takes what goes on in your mind and the decisions you make. If you want to change your world, first control what goes on in your mind.

You're very important to your generation. Rise and shine, rock your world and affect the environment around you.

Destiny Is A Matter Of Choice

Your parents believe in you and expect you to bring a better future to their tribe. You were born with a destiny to bring solutions to the world, to change people's lives and make the world a better place; you were not born by mistake.

You were not born just because your parents had sex and your mother became pregnant. You're not a biological mistake. You're not a product of a man and a woman who cannot exercise self-control upon their sexual feeling. You are a product of the Creator .You were in the mind of God before your mother and father knew each other.

When you were born, God had an initial plan for your life. God used your father and mother as a mode of transportation to bring you to this world to give you a chance to fulfil his plans and purposes for your life.

No matter who you are, where you were born, whether born out of rape or consensual sex, whether or not you have a mother or father alive or dead, whether or not you know who your parents are, you

Destiny Is A Matter Of Choice

have a destiny to fulfil because you were brought here for a purpose.

You're here with that background. Now, what's next?

Accept your situation and move forward with your life.

Destiny Is A Matter Of Choice

Life is a Story

I like to define a person's life as the plot in a story, movie or film where the person is the main character. Life is a story and you are the main character in it. You will discover that some of the characters in your story will be there from the start to the end. As your life continues some people will disappear or will no longer play an important part.

The reason is because they have played their role and you have to go on. That's how life is. In life you will lose some of your beloved ones, but that must not stop you from moving forward. You have to accept that they have fulfilled their part and you have fulfilled your part in their lives.

Now that they are gone, what is next? It is up to you to determine what to do with your life. You can come from any kind of background and have a great life. You were meant to be great. You're an agent of change. You can be a destiny changer. You were made to prosper, to move from

Destiny Is A Matter Of Choice

that poor background to a better one; from zero to hero.

You have to decide your path in life. What path are you taking? You can become like your parents who struggled for most of their lives or you can take a different path. What future are you creating for yourself?

The world is waiting for your decision.

Destiny Is A Matter Of Choice

How Choices Affect Our Destiny

Our lives are made up of every decision that we make from time to time. In every aspect of life we consider many options and decide on the best choice to make. So basically, life is a series of decision-making activities.

We begin everything by choosing. We decide everything from the little issues to the complex ones. Certain people and situations can contribute in a decision making, though at the end it is you yourself who'll always make the final decision. To sum it all up, a decision is a big factor in determining what the reality will most likely be. It will probably affect your future.

That's why it's necessary to think long and hard to assure yourself of a good outcome. An example of a good decision would be letting go of the hatred for someone and accepting friendship with him or her. This could probably result in a good relationship between the two people.

An example of a bad decision would be slacking and procrastinating the entire

Destiny Is A Matter Of Choice

school year. This decision will definitely put you in a difficult place.

Apparently, decision-making gives us a glance of what our near future could be. When we make a decision, our destiny is shaped. Good and bad outcomes are the result of the decisions that we made.

It's always a choice whether we want our future to be worth all the risks or to enjoy every moment of life, regardless of the consequences, to live for yourself or to live for others, to be sad or be happy, to live or to die.

Destiny Is A Matter Of Choice

Have a Purpose

Have a purpose; a dream for your life. Your purpose and the choices you make provide the direction that your life takes. As a child of destiny you should be on a mission that leads to the achievement of your goals.

Without a purpose, without direction, you will go nowhere in life. With purpose and direction you can see the mission and proceed on a worthwhile journey.

Dream or Plan

Some people only dream whereas others wake up, plan and work towards their objectives.

Things don't just happen by chance. Something has to be done in order for things to happen. As someone with a purpose, you must not deceive yourself. Whatever you want to achieve you must work for.

In South Africa there is a saying: "Nothing for Mahala" which means nothing for free. Whatever you wish to be or wish to achieve in life, you have to

Destiny Is A Matter Of Choice

work for. You must march in the direction that leads to your success. Don't take roads that lead anywhere else. Remember that how much you work will determine how much you succeed.

The input you supply and the method of processing will determine your output.

The black book says, "A man who works hard shall rule, his stomach shall never taste hunger. He shall be a leader. A lazy man shall die of hunger. He shall be a slave of his own friend. To sit upon your hand will cause your poverty."

This means that you have to work hard to bring your dreams, goals and plans into reality.

Be Cautious

There are times when we can relax because everything is going well. It's mostly when we feel that we are achieving our desires and all is well. Then we start to work less aggressively and are open to failure. Every level of life requires a certain amount of effort that will take you to the next success level.

Destiny Is A Matter Of Choice

Seeing where you're going doesn't mean that you have arrived there. Don't be too excited about the future that you're walking towards. Rather keep walking and working hard to make sure that you get to your destination.

Destiny Is A Matter Of Choice

Use of Time

Procrastination is the murderer of time. They say "Time wasted, never reign". The way you spend your time determines the kind of a future that you will have. Some people say that time is money. I say that, "time controls your destiny. It is too expensive to be wasted, but almost impossible to recover".

Don't let opportunities fade away from you. Don't spend your time on things that will not profit you. My High School Principal, Mr J. M. Shikwambana, once said, "Life is like a business and it's useless to live it without a profit and it's foolishness to run at a loss". Time is very important; respect it.

Your use of time can determine how successful you will be in the future. How you employ time will determine what you achieve. What do you spend your time mostly doing?

We are all given twenty four hours in a day. How many days have you lived? How many hours have you spent wisely? What have you achieved so far?

Destiny Is A Matter Of Choice

Work Hard

Our principal used to tell us "Study as though your life depends on studying only". Working hard is one of life principles that will bring your dreams, goals and plans into reality. Whatever you want to achieve, you must labour for it. You must sweat. There is no sweet without sweat. Always remember that.

How hard you work and how smart you work will determine how successful you will be in life.

Commitment

A young man once asked a rich man, who was successful financially, socially, spiritually, and materially, the exact secret of his success.

The rich man told him "Let's meet on the beach at 4 a.m. exactly and I will show you the secret to my success".

The young man was dressed up in a handsome suit and arrived exactly on time the following day.

The rich man told him "I want you to walk into the water until your whole body

Destiny Is A Matter Of Choice

is covered with water. When your whole body including your head is covered, then stay as long as you can in the water."

The young man stayed just 60 seconds under water and then came out. The rich man asked him one question: "When you were in the water, what did you want to do?"

The young man answered, "I wanted to breathe."

The rich man said "This is my secret. If you want to be successful in life, then in the same way you need to breathe to survive, you need to work hard every second to be successful."

What made the man rich is that he spent all of his spare time working. His hard work made him into a billionaire.

Be willing to work hard in order to be successful in life. Be willing to pay the price of greatness. You may have to sacrifice some pleasures of life such as not being extravagant.

Destiny Is A Matter Of Choice

Measure Your Success

There was once a swimming competition for which in order to win you had to swim 1000 metres across a river. One of the competitors was leading after swimming half way across the river. At this point, he stopped and said, "I am quitting. I am too tired to continue." He decided to return to the starting point.

As a result, he swam the same distance as he would have in order to win the race. When he realized that, he wished he had completed the race. It was too late. Others had already completed their race.

The race is the journey of your life and the metres are the measure of how much you have to work in order to be successful in life or how much far you have to walk to fulfil your destiny.

Don't Quit

Do not quit on your life. You can make it. Why not? What about the others who have made it? They are just like you. Life is not all about having the whole world in your hand. It's all about trying your best to do

Destiny Is A Matter Of Choice

all that you can in order to be a successful person.

Don't quit on the way to your destiny.

Don't quit on reaching the goals you wish to achieve in life. Things will not always be in the manner you wish. Learn to accept what happens and move forward. Quitting makes you feel that you're a failure, a loser, a fallen hero, even a useless hopeless thing. Remember you're the light of the world and people are pulling for you.

We are all role models for others. Some people are going to follow our every step. Don't disappoint the children. Be strong; move on. Men of vision do not die easily. You can't afford to lose. It is more difficult to live with a failure than to move forward towards your success.

Life seems to be hard with many difficult situations, but always know that the present is not necessarily the conclusion of your destiny. You can continue to make progress and overcome a desire to quit.

Destiny Is A Matter Of Choice

See The Future

My Pastor, C.A. Emmanuel, used to say this: "What you see is what you will possess". Seeing where you are going and having a vision of the future, helps you to concentrate on the things you ought to achieve in life. Plan your life. If you fail to plan, you have already planned to fail.

If you don't decide the type of future you desire or life objectives to be achieved, then nature will decide for you. As a person of purpose, I know where I come from and I know where I am going. Do you?

Who are you? What does the future have for you?

How far do you want to go in life? What do you want to achieve?

Destiny Is A Matter Of Choice

Avoid Destiny Robbers

Destiny robbers are people who don't have anything to do in life. They betray, criticize, destroy and steal the destiny of others.

When you are at the top, people will talk about you. Ignore what people say. As a leader, you have the skills to climb the ladder to the top. You know yourself better than others do. Remember that they see only your actions, but do not know how you are within. The real you is within. They don't know your gifts, talents and your abilities. They will describe you by where you come from, not by where you're going.

Sometimes people judge you by what you wear. You should dress appropriately for the task at hand, but not worry if others don't like it. "Don't judge a book by its cover" is a suitable admonition.

Don't be discouraged by what people say about you. You know yourself better than they do.

Destiny Is A Matter Of Choice

Always try to move forward and improve yourself. You know who you are; where you come from and where you're going.

Motivate Yourself

You are your own best motivator. Motivation that comes from others can be useful especially if they are your mentors.

Learn to say positive things about your life. Always tell yourself that you can and will make it in life. Don't listen to what negative people say to you.

Be careful of what goes into your mind. People can be poisonous .They can poison your intention by what they say and turn you into a failure. They might know where you come from, but they don't know where you're going or who you will become.

Follow your own path because you are not on the same mission as they are.

Mistakes

We all make mistakes. All in all you have to learn from your mistakes and tell yourself that you will not commit the same mistake again. If you make a

Destiny Is A Matter Of Choice

mistake and you make it again, it's no longer a mistake. It has become a choice that you have taken knowingly.

The best thing is to forgive yourself and move forward with your life. You can help others by revealing your mistakes and showing how to avoid them.

My Principal once said, "If your parents have built a ten-room house and you have built one that has less than ten rooms, you're a failure. You are supposed to show that the next generation can rise to a higher level".

When he said this, what came to my mind was "repetition of mistakes". Sometimes we commit the same mistakes in life that our parents and ancestors have committed.

Remember this is all about destiny; it's all about the matter of making your own choice in life.

Our parents provide a great example of the result of choices that they have made in life. We must learn from them. They are where they are because of the choices they have made. They made their choices and their destiny resulted. So will it be for

Destiny Is A Matter Of Choice

you. Consider what made them what they are today. Be careful not to make the same mistakes they have made, if any.

Some mistaken decisions are so serious that they prevent you from achieving the destiny you sought.

Some mistakes can be corrected. However, some mistaken decisions put you on the wrong path and cannot be remedied.

Whatever you do, whatever decisions or choices you make, set yourself on a path in the same way as planting a particular seed will produce a specific crop.

My mother had a plan for her life that she was unable to follow because she became pregnant at the age of sixteen and had to drop out of school to take care of me. She told me this so that I might not commit the same mistake. Of course, as a male, I'm unlikely to become pregnant, but as a responsible person, if I happened to get a young lady pregnant, I would have to make major changes in my life and the plan for my destiny would be delayed and altered significantly.

Destiny Is A Matter Of Choice

My mother was able to move forward with her life and now she is happily married with four children. I do not blame her or feel ashamed of her because of that experience. I am proud of her. After all, I am here because of her decision not to have an abortion.

I mention this to show you how the power of a mistake can operate on a tribe or generation. Many families have similar experiences.

My mother told me everything I had to know about sex, unplanned pregnancy, and how to live a good life. When I was sixteen years old I had decided and made the choice that history would not repeat itself upon me and my generation. I have set an example for my future generations.

Some mistakes can affect you for the rest of your life. Therefore, make decisions carefully and avoid making serious mistakes. Five minutes of pleasure can result in a lifetime of regret.

Destiny Is A Matter Of Choice

Who Can Destroy Your Destiny?
Friendly Enemies

Friendly enemies are those who are close to you, who may even be your best friends, but who try to lead you from the path you are following. These people may encourage you to do wrong things that happen to make you feel good. Remember not everything that makes you feel good, is good.

Friendly enemies will never tell you that what you are doing is wrong even if it is. They will not encourage you to do anything good. Mostly they pretend to be grateful to be your friend, but they are jealous and they envy you. Their mission is to influence you to do things that will end up destroying your life.

They lead you to do things that could terminate your life or destiny. They try to change your purpose and give you a negative one. They try to change your direction to one that leads to destruction.

Remember friends can be more influential than your parents, your spouse or your mentor.

Destiny Is A Matter Of Choice

Who are your friends? Show me your friends and I will tell you who you are by judging their character.

Bad Company

The bible says that, "Bad company corrupts good manners."

The people with whom you live can determine what you become in life. The ones who are closest to you and are effective in giving you advice can control your destiny. Students generally spend more time with their friends than with family members or religious leaders.

They say, "Birds of a feather flock together."

They say, "Influence them before they influence you, and do unto them before they do unto you,"

In life you have to watch the kind of company that you keep. Do your friends influence you negatively or positively? Do they give directions that lead to more success in life?

If you hang around with people who are not concerned about life and prosperity,

Destiny Is A Matter Of Choice

but simply drift as the whim takes them one way or another, you will become like them. If you decide to be close to those who perform well in school, you are bound to do well yourself.

Some people are bad. They live without a purpose and they are going nowhere in life. If you live with them, they will kill your vision also. Separate yourself from bad company or they will corrupt your life.

Have you ever heard someone saying, 'I hate myself?" I hope you don't want to be in the same situation by not making a right choice on the company you keep. Stay out of trouble and trouble will not trouble you; but if you trouble trouble, trouble will trouble you.

Destiny Is A Matter Of Choice

Use Your Time and Money Effectively

Most people who are successful in life sacrifice a lot and don't waste their time or money on unnecessary things.

Time

Let me start with time. If you are extravagant with your time, you're not likely to become most successful in life.

Most successful people set their goals and plan how they will achieve them. They often plan their day, allotting time according to the importance or urgency of the task. At the end of the day, they review what they have accomplished and write down the tasks for the next day.

We are all given twenty four hours a day in which we eat, sleep, plan, work and relax. What do you do with your time? Some people need more sleep than others so they have to be more effective in planning and working.

At the end of each day, when you try to account for your time, ask yourself if you have used your time effectively. Did you achieve your day's objectives?

Destiny Is A Matter Of Choice

You can waste your valuable time by watching too much TV or by sleeping longer than you need to.

Money

Most people think that they have achieved success when they graduate from university and get a job.

However, being an employee is only a starting point. If your goal is to become rich, you will need to be an employer, not an employee. You need to find a suitable business that you can own, manage and develop.

Now that you are working and employed, think of something that you can do that will give you a greater profit. Look at businesses and invest your savings wisely. Don't spend all your excess money on pleasure. Some people had nothing when they started; but because they sacrificed and invested well, today they are rich.

Don't be extravagant. Don't spend your money on luxury. With many small investments over a long period of time you can become a millionaire. Ask yourself what can you start with the small

Destiny Is A Matter Of Choice

amount of money you have available that can take you to another level of success.

Don't spend your money on clothes and electronics that are not essential. Rather use it for things that will profit you.

Destiny Is A Matter Of Choice

Seek Advice

We all make mistakes, but some people can anticipate the mistakes we can make before we make them and they can suggest to us how to avoid the mistakes. Accept these reminders and corrections. It is foolish to reject good advice. If you wish to continue to improve, you need to love getting advice and be disciplined enough to follow it.

If you're a person who hates being corrected by others, you will not make it in life. After all, you cannot know everything. Your education will continue until you die. There is a saying, "An old man sitting under the shadow of a tree sees farther than a young man standing upon a hill."

We need mentors and advisors in life. People with experience can teach us and guide us in the right direction. Sometimes their advice can come in the form of a rebuke. To be rebuked is not sweet, but it helps us and saves from destruction. Love to be corrected and you will never be lost.

Destiny Is A Matter Of Choice

Things You Need

These are some of the things you need for your journey through life.

- *A pencil and a diary*
- *A Rubber*
- *A compass*
- *A chair*

Now you may ask yourself why carry a pencil and a diary along, Mr Blessed? A pencil is to remind you that you can always start a new page of your life. The diary is to remind you that you can always start afresh by tearing a page and start a new one.

This means that you can always find another way to lead to your success.

You may ask why carry along a rubber, Mr Blessed? A rubber is to remind you that we all can make mistakes, but you can let go of the past and move forward.

Again you may ask why carry a compass, Mr Blessed? A compass gives you direction. It indicates different directions and you choose your direction. A

Destiny Is A Matter Of Choice

compass is to remind you of your direction and the purpose of where you're going.

Lastly you wonder why carry a chair along. A chair simply means a position. It is to remind you of your purpose. It is to remind you who you are, where you come from and where you're going. It reminds you of how far have you walked and achieved upon your life and destiny.

Destiny Is A Matter Of Choice

Be Single-Minded

As you go along the journey of your life you will meet dogs that will bark at you. Do not pay attention to them. Not every dog that barks at you will bite. Some dogs just bark to get attention and to make you lose concentration on your journey.

You're In Charge Of Your Destiny

As we continue to live our lives, it's up to us to decide our tomorrow. The way we live will determine how life will respond to us. Who we are as people and what we choose to get out of life are equally important and they can affect us in a positive or negative ways.

The result of the choices that I made will decide my destiny. My destiny lies in my own hand. It's up to me to decide the kind of outcomes I want for my life.

I believe that if you have a dream or an objective, you can easily make it come true. Having confidence in yourself is the first step. Having a positive mind will help you to have positive outcomes. Make your life what you want it to be and the rest shall fall into place.

Destiny Is A Matter Of Choice

Life is too short to be wasted. You live once and die once and good opportunities tend to be few, sometimes occurring only once in a lifetime. Your future is yours and you have the right to control it.

Instead of concentrating on your past or mistakes, construct a positive being within yourself by changing your mind. Recognise your mistakes and learn from them. Leave worries behind and go where you think it is rightfully yours in your life.

Succeeding is not a hard task. You can succeed as long as you make up your mind never to allow negative thoughts, influences and sayings pull you down. Be proud of who you are and control your own destiny. Make your own choices about your life and your choices will make you.

Remember your destiny is in your hand.

Destiny Is A Matter Of Choice

Why Some People Fail To Fulfil Their Destiny

As a person with a purpose, the most important thing is to fulfil your destiny by reaching your destiny objectives. Many people fail to fulfil their destiny and turn into someone they never intended or wanted to be.

When it comes to your goals, your mission and vision, who do you want to be or what do you want to achieve? It is what you see that you will possess. When an individual sets goals they tend to be wealth goals or goals to achieve a career which is the first step in prosperity.

Here are twelve reasons why many people fail to fulfil their destiny:

- *Fear of success and/failure.*
- *Lack of understanding upon achieving their objectives setting process*
- *Lack of commitment to their objectives*
- *Stagnation*
- *Questions and doubts*

Destiny Is A Matter Of Choice

- *Lack of a real destination*
- *Failing to plan*
- *Having too many goals*
- *Feeling unworthy of the outcomes*
- *Lack of motivation*
- *Lack of consistency*
- *Excuses*

Fear of success and failure

Some people are afraid they will fail or even worse that they will actually succeed. As a result they don't bother to take the steps to achieve their objectives.

Such people lack belief in themselves and their potential.

They think that if they fail, everyone will have a negative thought about them. It is because of their mind set and the kind of nature in them that makes them not take a step forward.

Realize that you can achieve anything you set your mind to when you focus. Believe in yourself and your abilities and others will too. After all, to fail does not mean you're a failure. You become a failure only when you stop trying.

Destiny Is A Matter Of Choice

The fact that you are still on the battleground proves that you're not a failure.

Most people who are great in life today have failed once, but they did not give up. If someone is making it now it does not mean they will end up making it in life. Only if they are focused enough will they succeed.

Some people are good in education or their profession, but when it comes to life in general they have failed already. It's not about how you start it's about how you end.

Lack of understanding upon achieving their objectives-setting process

Many people mistakenly believe that setting objectives means putting a goal statement on a paper, setting a completion date, making check mark and starting all over again.

Such a mind-set is wrong and it hinders people from prospering. The setting of goals and scratching them off and starting over again is like a student who changes a course every year at the university.

Destiny Is A Matter Of Choice

Setting a goal does not change you. When you achieve a goal, you have changed because of the accomplishment. Goals are not short quick things; they are fixed and immovable destinations that show the world who you are and what you want to become or achieve. Objectives can be thought of as steps towards a goal.

Therefore, fully dedicate yourself to achieving your objectives if you want to reach your destination.

Lack of commitment to their objectives

Many people state that they want to achieve a goal. In truth, they're really not committed to it Because of this lack of commitment they do not give objective attainment their full effort.

As with anything in life, if you do not commit all your strength to the task, you will be disappointed. The kind of input you apply and the method of your processing will determine your outcome. Commit yourself to any goal or objective that you want to achieve.

Commitment is crucial for attaining any objective.

Destiny Is A Matter Of Choice

Stagnation

After setting a goal, writing down dates and setting checkpoints, some people stop moving forward towards their success in fulfilment of their destiny goals.

They never actually take the first step needed to progress. Realize that if you don't get started you can't go anywhere.

Without action nothing happens. So if you created an objective about your life and destiny and wonder why nothing has changed, ask yourself what steps have you taken to achieve that objective. If you haven't started yet, now is the time.

Questions and doubts

Many people let questions and doubts paralyze them. They believe they can't start on a goal of fulfilling their destiny until they have all the answers to every "what if". However no matter how long and hard you prepare, you will never have all the answers to the questions you ask.

You have to know that life will not always be as you wish. Most people make their choices and answer their questions based

Destiny Is A Matter Of Choice

on where they are right now rather than on where they want to go or who they want to become.

Always base your choices, questions and answers with a view to the future, not in view of the current situation for your current situation is not your conclusion.

Your situation will change because of the choices you make today and will affect the success of your journey. So move forward with your life towards achieving your objectives and fulfilling your destiny. Know that you will never have all the answers to your question.

Lack of a real destination

People often begin setting a goal without a solid understanding of who they are, who they want to become, or what they ultimately want to achieve. If you don't have a destination in mind, then you'll never know which road to take to get to your destination.

Your destination needs to be clear. It must be something you can visualize and explain to others. Without such a clear

Destiny Is A Matter Of Choice

view of what you want in life; you'll forever be changing course and falling short of your potential. It may also lead you to be extravagant in other areas of your life.

Failing to plan

While many people understand the formula of objective setting and the formula to achieve, they don't have a plan for goal attainment that is personalized to them and their experiences of life. In other words, they fail by neglecting the talent, gifts and abilities they possess which can help them attain the objectives of their destiny.

As well, they fail to use the people they know who may help them plan and achieve their objectives. We each bring so many unique talents and attributes to the table and we know a multitude of people who can help us in some way.

Wisely seek guidance from mentors and people who have being successful in the direction you're taking and plan on how you will reach your destination. If you fail to plan you have already planned to fail.

Destiny Is A Matter Of Choice

Having too many goals

Some people have too many goals and not enough focus on any one goal. It's as though they are standing in front of a dart board with three targets in mind.

Hitting just one target is difficult enough; hitting all three targets with one dart is impossible. Therefore, determine the main one to be focused on and move forward with that one goal only. Eliminate other goals or put them aside for now.

This is not to say you should never have more than one goal. You can't do many things in the same time and with the same target. Rather you need to realize that you have only a limited time and should choose the goal that will give you the highest achievement for your effort. Once a goal is achieved, your next step is to focus on the other goals in sequence. Make sure you balance all your life activities while pursuing the goals.

Feeling unworthy of the outcomes

Some people really don't believe they can become great or worthy of attaining their objectives. As a result, they sabotage

Destiny Is A Matter Of Choice

themselves. They suddenly walk away from the key person who could help them with their goals. They let all the life opportunities fade away from them.

They neglect to do a critical activity that will enable them to achieve their destiny goals.

People who feel unworthy usually lack confidence in themselves. They don't believe in themselves. Confidence is the key point to objective attainment in destiny.

Lack of motivation

Many people are satisfied with what they have and where they are in life. As a result they don't explore what else is available or what greater things they could achieve or accomplish.

Our motivation changes our pain and pleasure in a situation. That's why we need mentors and people who will help us advance from one level to the next.

If someone is feeling pain in a situation, that pain may not be great enough to make the person strive for more. That's why

Destiny Is A Matter Of Choice

mentors tell us there is no gain without pain.

Change and objective attainment will happen only when you are ready to break the present status and strive for better.

Finally, fulfilling your destiny goals is possible. You can really be who you want to be and do what you want to do, by balancing your goals and avoiding every obstacle and mistake that hinders getting the desired result.

You can achieve any goal you set for yourself and reach a new level of personal and professional success in life in your destiny.

Lack of consistency

Life is not going to be the way we want it to be all the time. Trials will come and events that will try to pull us down will come our way. Tell yourself that you're going to make it in life. Be consistent in doing all the things that will escort you to your destination.

If you're not consistent enough in walking towards your achievement, you're not

Destiny Is A Matter Of Choice

likely to reach your destination. Be consistent in working hard and in making right choices and you will achieve your greatness.

Excuses

Excuses are the greatest enemies of destiny. If you want make it in life, you must avoid making excuses. Be responsible enough in carrying out your plans and duties as you're supposed to without wasting time by always postponing your plans.

You're the one who has to work for what you want. If you run away from responsibility you will achieve nothing. Don't be lazy. Laziness will bring you poverty. You don't have a reason why you shouldn't make it in life.

They say there many ways to skin a cat. To me they are saying that there are different ways of becoming successful in life.

So you don't have any excuse for why you can't make it because you have many options and many opportunities. Destiny is a matter of choice. Make your choice

Destiny Is A Matter Of Choice

and your choice will make you. To choose nothing will make you nothing.

Destiny Is A Matter Of Choice

Enemies of destiny

In life as you fulfil your destiny, you will face many questionable situations and you'll have to overcome powerful negative thoughts which might come in the form of challenges emotionally, struggles and hopelessness.

These enemies of destiny oppose you every day. They emerge from your past to steal your future. They dilute your ability to love and trust and feel safe especially when you are disappointed. They paralyze your confidence to move ahead in fulfilling God's perfect will for your life. If you don't fight against these enemies of destiny, they will pull you down.

As a person aiming to reach your destination, you must overcome every challenge you come across such as hopelessness, disappointment and things that stand as obstacles in your life.

Overcome the enemies of your destiny by putting an end to the following:

- ***The fear of trusting others.*** For we all need destiny helpers.

Destiny Is A Matter Of Choice

- ***The expectation of betrayal.***

In the organisation I am mentoring, I have being betrayed and criticised many times even by the people I trusted, but I didn't let fear of being in the same situation prevent me from going forward.

I just accepted that it's part of life. As you know, when you're at the top you become a topic. I made sure as the one in charge, as the chairperson, that the organisation still achieved its objectives.

- ***The feeling that people will let you down.***

Yes, people may let you down. Your destiny is not in the hands of anyone. Always tend to move forward.

- ***The sensation of facing everything alone.***

Life is a battle. If you don't fight, you will be attacked. You have to stand. You were born alone. Remember that a crown has one head position. Fight for your crown.

- ***The expectation that things will go wrong.***

Destiny Is A Matter Of Choice

Yes, things might go wrong, but there is a solution to every problem and in every wrestling match, there is a victor.

There was once a man who had a farm. He had all sorts of fruit and vegetables in his farm.

During the time of harvest, he always harvested less than he expected, because before he sent his workers to the fields he had a great amount of fruit hanging on the trees. As he used to walk in the gardens, he knew that his harvest was great. But he always reaped less than expected. His labourers were stealing from the harvest.

So the owner of the farm came up with a plan. He installed security cameras which his workers were not aware of. He called a meeting and gave instruction and travelled abroad to overseas.

The workers were so happy. They started stealing fruit and vegetables, but the cameras were recording every event as they were wisely installed.

When the owner came back, he saw all the events that had taken place and recognised all the thieves in his farm. He called them

Destiny Is A Matter Of Choice

all and showed them the video. They were embarrassed and they got what they deserved. He sacked them.

- ### *The fear of death*

Men of vision don't die easily.

There was once a man who worked in a butchery firm. His master loved him so much because he was a loyal and obedient servant. His fellow colleagues hated him because he always reported them when they stole.

They hated him mostly because he was highly loved by his master. His vision was to become in charge of the others as a form of promotion.

The workers planned to kill this man. One day he was in a fridge packing meat there. They locked him in the fridge. Later on, their master was looking for him, but he was nowhere to be found.

In the fridge he realised he would not survive if he remained in one spot. He placed himself into duty. He carried the meat changing the positions from left to right.

Destiny Is A Matter Of Choice

As he was a hard worker, he worked the whole time in the fridge. He did not rest or sleep. He kept himself busy until the following day.

In the morning when his enemies came, they opened the fridge and he was alive. When the master found what they had done, he punished the others and promoted him to his vision.

- ***The fear of not taking risk.***

It is a risk not to take as risk.

The Creator has made you into an incredible being of life that leads into ultimate abundant greatness. There is a victor within you. Face every enemy of life and destiny. Betrayal, abundant fear, hopelessness, and failure are not your portion. Destiny is a matter of choice.

Destiny Is A Matter Of Choice

Fulfil your destiny

The ultimate goal of all creatures is to make it to the future. The greatest tragedy in life is premature termination of destiny.

Remember destiny is:

- The reason for your existence
- The original purpose or mission and vision to be achieved by you.

Be honest with yourself. Reality will always be real and the truth will never be proven wrong. Make your own choice and your choice will make you. If you're not sincere with your life, you will continue to battle problems and never be victorious.

In the journey of life they are many voices speaking to you. Be wary of which ones you obey. Obey the voice of your purpose of existence and fulfil your destiny.

www.ingramcontent.com/pod-product-compliance
Lightning Source LLC
Chambersburg PA
CBHW061252040426
42444CB00010B/2363